Poems from the Heart

By Karen Farmer

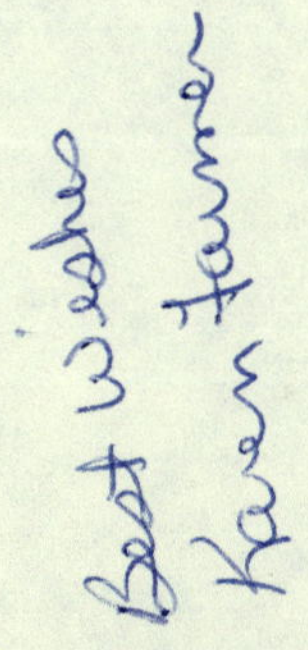

Publisher: Ralph Roberts

Executive Editor: Kathryn L. Hall

Production Editor: Melody A. Grandy

Cover Design: WorldComm®

Interior Design and Electronic Page Assembly: WorldComm®

Printed in the United States of America

10 9 8 7 6 5 4 3 2 1

ISBN 1-56664-032-6

WorldComm Press—a Division of Creativity, Inc., 65 Macedonia Road, Alexander, North Carolina 28701, (704) 252-9515—is a full service publisher.

Dedicated to:

Chris my son,
that special light in my
life that forever keeps me
out of darkness.

Lynn,
my dear friend
for over half my life
who believed in
and
only saw
the good in
me.

Acknowledgements:

Sandy and Kim, for believing in me and my work and making me strong enough to try.

Simone, for continously pushing me into doing what I wanted and for giving me that famous "attitude adjustment" when needed.

Tootie and Mildred, for their love and undying faith.

Karen, for showing me there are still good people in the world.

Judy, for being there when I needed her.

Melba, Julie, and Missy; and Keith, Carl, and Freddy, just because they cared.

Mrs. Cox, my teacher, my friend, for making me take pride in everything I do.

Patsy, just because.

To Vickie, thanks for being an inspiration and a friend.

For E.C.G, without whom my dream would still just be a dream.

And to all the many friends I've met & made along the way. Thanks to each of you for the greatest gift of all; your love and support. Because of your support, I have accomplished my dream.

Contents

Special

A Locket and A Diary

Hey, I found a locket, I once heard someone say
It seems that it was found on a cold wintery day
Inside the locket was a picture of someone standing bold
It was of a lady who seemed to be quite old
There was a great mystery to this locket that was found
So I began detecting upon the sacred ground
I found a faded diary; its lettering was intact
Even though I shouldn't read it, I just couldn't put it back
I drifted off into a world unlike the one I know
Where flowers seem to dance and faces seemed to glow
As I read on a little further, I was soon to find
How one lady's dreams gave her peace of mind
It told of personal things which I felt I shouldn't read
Of how you get much warmth just from doing a good deed
It began telling of love and all its hurts
Even told about a time she sewed someone's shirt
It told of her life and all the pleasures in it
Even how she seemed to laugh each and every minute
As I kept on reading I found some sadness, too
She spoke of death and all the things that can make you blue
Then she told about a locket that she gave to a man
It seemed that he wore it tied around his hand
Then one day he lost it, along with his pride
Because the locket kept him going, it was always by his side
She told of a religion that kept them apart
How her folks wouldn't let them marry, it really broke her heart
It tells how she searched for that locket, that was so very dear
She felt like if she found it, he would always be near
Then the writing gets lighter as she speaks of being grey
She goes on to tell "It feels awful cold today."
I think I'll just go to sleep now and wait on the birds
For it seems with their chirping, they're saying kind words
They always wake me up at the crack of dawn
Asking for a piece of bread and just making sure I'm home

Animals

You can see many animals if you go to the zoo
Every once in a while you can pet one or two
But those aren't the best, or even man's best friend
I like the kind you can hold in your hand
How about the kitten so cuddly and soft
Or the little chicks you find in the loft
Horses are fun to watch, running wild and free
But dogs are better, as they'll play with me
We can see cows down on the farm
Pigs playing in the mud; roosters in the barn
Ducks out on the lake; butterflies in the air
Spiders on the fence post; flies everywhere
Birds are pretty and easy to take care of
Rabbits are cute critters and hard not to love
Monkeys are special; zebras with their stripes
Goats drinking from a bottle; snakes that don't bite
Gerbils in a cage; goldfish in a bowl
Some are pretty ugly, like the old black mole
There are lots of animals, but never have I yet
Found any I like better than the ones that make a pet

Whales

Whales are such a mystery
Living deep within the sea
The largest mammal so they say
Warm blooded in a natural way
A coat of blubber to keep warm
The sea an umbrella for a storm
Their skin is as smooth as silk
Their tummies are as white as milk
Let's take a whale on a date
I have a feeling, it will be great
Come on, let's go inside
What a great place to hide
A fast cruise across the sea
The best part is, it's free

Surface to the top for some air
Then down below to see what's there
Caviar for breakfast, doesn't cost a dime
We could have it all the time
A water spout near the brain
Showers will never be the same
Glide through the water like a jet
I think I'd like one for a pet
Since that's impossible for you or me
At least we solved the mystery...

Unicorns

Unicorns are special
With a horn in the center of their face
It gives them a great beauty
Of much style and grace

They're something little girls dream on
As they fly through the night
The darkness doesn't matter
With their skin shining bright

Unicorns are magical
A mystery to relate
I'd love to see one standing
Beside the garden gate

A horse of such beauty
All white and standing tall
I'm sure glad I have one
Hanging on the wall.

Mirrors

I look in the mirror and what do I see
My own reflection's looking back at me
A mirror holds your secrets, oh the stories it could tell
Especially all the times you weren't looking very well
Your reflection on the other side is anything you please
As your imagination is what the eye sees
You can be a princess, a model, or a star
Even the town drunk just home from the bar
A mirror is a special friend; you share with it your scorn
At how very bad you look in the early morn
It knows of your beauty when you're dressed to go out at night
Even about the black eye you obtained in a fight
You share with it your hairdo; the pimple on your chin
The way you plan to make eyes at all the good looking men
A mirror gets the practice for your very first kiss
Gets to see the sadness at the one you missed
You use it to check the puffiness all around your eyes
One thing is for certain a mirror never lies
It is used quite often for checking fat around your waist
Guess that's why we have them hanging all over the place
Most people have one with them everywhere they go
It holds your picture in rain and in snow
Run out and get one; keep it close at hand
It will make you feel as though you have a special friend

Love

Lonely nights
Ordered around
Very sorry for things done wrong
Eternity

All of this rolled into one
Is something we've all done
If you've ever been in love
With the knowledge from above
We'll bear with it every day
'Cause real love is this way

Memories

Memories are something that lingers
Whether they're good or bad
Sometimes they make you happy
Other times they make you sad

I remember the first day of school
My lunch was in a sack
I remember when the bell rang
I swore I'd never come back

I remember getting older
At last becoming a teen
I could never remember
The years that were in between

I remember graduation
Sitting by a boy named Mac
And to think that after my first day
I hadn't wanted to come back

Soon we were off to college
To make our future plans
It was only the girls though
The guys were fighting for our land

Now I'm a lot older
And can't recall too well
All the childhood dreams
We promised not to tell

Our memories carry on
Even though we pass away
I'm glad I shared them with you
On such a pretty day

You've heard my memories now
Add them to your own
As they start from your childhood
And continue when you're grown

Children

Little people's laughter everywhere
Running around without a care
Sometimes lost and all alone
Walking slow on their way home
Cuts and bruises always hurt
Little girls in Mommy's skirt
Little boys with ball and bat
Don't forget the cowboy hat
Looking up with shining eyes
At the wonder in the skies
A kite flying on a windy day
Wishing when it rains they could go out to play
Swimming in the summer time
Thoughts of winter on their mind
Sleigh riding in the snow
With their cheeks all aglow
Hot chocolate by an open fire
Wishing for their heart's desire
Growing up is such a hard task
Becoming a grown up at last
Then the cycle starts again
Of the little women and men
All the hopes and dreams
Of happiness and life schemes
Growing up with a family of your own
Keeping the cycle going strong

My Brother

My brother isn't very loving
Well not as loving as I am
But at times he says such sweet things
That would knock you to the ground

The other day I asked what kind of mother he thought I'd be
Well his answer made my eyes flood
He said, "You know you'll be a good one
For you have our Mother's blood"

That brought a chill over me
That I can't describe
And yet at the same time
It made me warm inside

He was never much on speeches
Words don't come easily
But on that summer day
He was a great author to me

I'll never forget our talk
On that sunny day
My brother was saying he loved me
In a very special way

To My Little Girl

As I watch you grow older I'm hoping one day
The Lord will take hold of you and show you the way
I've done all I can here in this life
I've carried you through the pain and the strife
I've given you all a Mother can give
For I promised that when you came to live
In my heart I carried you through
Promised you'd never have to be blue
I'll be leaving you soon; I have to go on
For the Lord called and said, "It's time to go home"
I hate to leave you, but I know I must
But I'll leave with the Lord; in Him I trust
He'll finish the job I started so many years ago
I'll be in heaven watching you grow
When you get older and have children of your own
The Lord will bless them and your home
I'm leaving my love and the knowledge of the Lord
Within your heart I hope you have stored
All of our memories old and new
And remember, my child, don't ever be blue
For the Lord will be with you; I'll watch from above
Sending you down all of my love

Service Life and A Service Wife

You're gone now, but only for a while
You left me here with a smile
The family was there you said your good-byes
You were holding me close with your eyes
"I have to go and serve my time
For the country they say is mine
I'm off to a land across the sea
Helping our country to remain free"
I can hardly wait for your return
I want to hear all you've learned
There's so much for us to catch up on
I'll be glad when you return home
The days are moving by real fast
You'll soon be home at last
And even though we're miles apart
Our love keeps us close at heart

The Magic of Love

Love found her on the street
Only by chance the two should meet
She wouldn't have known if it hadn't been
for his twinkling eyes and his magic grin
They fell in love from the start
And then he began breaking her heart
She began to hate all things around
But decided to search for a love like she'd once found
She found it waiting at her door
There to stay forever more
Never again would she lose this love
For it was sent from heaven above
Put in her heart; there to stay
Till eternity comes their way

Dreams

My life is full of dreams
Of great happiness and sun beams
At least I have something to look forward to
I have lots of things to do
You see I have a little boy
Who has filled my heart with joy
For him I have many hopes
For this reason I cannot mope
I must fulfill my dreams
Life is hard so it seems
But we'll make it, him and I
Our dreams will carry us to the sky
We'll climb mountains and reach the sun
Something no one else has ever done
There'll be battles, but we'll win
So his life will be free from sin
I love you so my little boy
Your Mommy's favorite toy
You'll have your dreams as you grow old
Carry them, they're an easy load
I know all your dreams will come true
'Cause this is what I've dreamed for you

That First Day

The first day I saw you
I knew from the very start
That I'd fallen in love
'Cause I could feel it in my heart

Our love is so special to me
It's so hard to explain
And the magic of it all
Is knowing you feel the same

Can you understand how I feel
I sincerely hope you do
Guess what I'm trying to say is
That I'm madly in love with you

Feelings

Have you ever wondered what it feels like
To think that no one cares
And feel out of place
Or that there's no one to share

You can't seem to find a friend
To lend a listening ear
'Cause it seems when you have problems
No one wants to hear

Have you ever been lonely
Or felt that you were blue
When you have a lot to worry about
And no one's around but you

Have you ever thought of how it would be
To know someone would always be there
And whenever a problem came about
You'd have someone with whom to share

Have you ever wanted someone
When times were really rough
And know in your heart
They realize you're not so tough

Have you ever thought of how it would be
If your friends were there without your asking
And know they'd always be there
'Cause their friendship's everlasting

Give some thought to these things
And if you haven't, start
Check and see if your friendship
Comes from the bottom of your heart

What Is Love

Love is many things:

Sometimes quiet, sometimes gay
A happy feeling that everything's okay
It's understanding in a thousand little ways
Knowing at the right moment exactly what to say
A smile across a crowded room, a touch, a tender kiss
When you're going away saying it's you I'm gonna miss
Love is knowing when to say it in a gentle way
Remember it doesn't matter the exact time of day
A voice of reassurance or a word of praise
Knowing when to say, there will be better days
Love is for many people both big and small
I know the Lord sent it to us one and all
I fell in love, never had I known such bliss
And found that nothing else could bring me happiness
To be honest, I never knew
What love was until I fell in love with you
Oh, I've had romantic notions, but none of them were real
As I've never had this feeling that I suddenly feel
As there's so much to our love and the more I learn about it
I find that there's just no way I could ever live without it

Chance Meeting

Love found them on the street
Only by chance that they should meet
But once they looked into each other's eyes
Something like magic must have fallen from the skies
They knew they had fallen for each other
And it's not the love you'd give to a brother
It was a special love shared only by two
It's the love God wants for you
The love that makes you want to stay
By each other's side, every day

Lost Love

A soft voice that sounds so sweet
His looks are, oh, so very neat
We shared a love that was great
Neither one of us could hardly wait
Then all of a sudden he met someone new
My world became empty and blue
How could a love so real
Become so distant and still
I always think of the love we had
It makes me so unhappy and mad
To think I didn't put up a fight
For what I felt was really right
But as I said, "I want only your happiness"
Then if you are, I will bless
The life and love that you chose
Knowing that you wanted those
Just remember one thing my dear
I'll always hold our memories near

Cupid

Cupid shot me with his arrow
And I know that it was real
Because of the love and warmth
That I began to feel

It's weird, though,
How sneaky cupid is
He sneaks up behind you
And claims that you're his

And then he gives you a shot
And the guy you're looking at
Becomes the love of your life
Just like that

Love

Dream Come True

When my love and I are together
It's like a dream come true
We're living in a world made up
Of just us two

We always let time pass us by
For that is all we've got
We know it will last forever
As we sure do have a lot

For now no one knows of my crime
But I'm sure they'll find it out
Especially if there's watchful eyes
Always lurking about

I may get twenty years
For this love I stole
But hopefully I'll be out
Before I get too old

We could go on forever
Without being found
As long as we're careful
When we meet downtown

Our love grows with each day
It shows with every glance
Now I must tell you something
While I have the chance

I love you more and more each day
In a very special way

Loving you has brought a meaning
To life that I cannot hide
Without this love of ours
I know I couldn't survive

So in this poem I'm telling you
How much I love you, dear
And how I'm always wishing
That you were here

You should never have to wonder
If my love for you is real

As in this poem I've told you
How I truly feel

For now I am closing
And going on my way
Remember that I love you more
With each passing day

Love

Love is something wonderful and good
It's so great, everyone should
Have some of it to pass around
I'm sure if you look it can be found
Look in the eyes of the one you love
And if they shine like the stars above
You'll know he loves you in return
And that you're his only concern
Love can be shown in many ways
But it's best if you show it every day
The best love is the one shared by two
When you care if your mate is blue
When you know in your heart that you both care
And in each other's life you want to share
That's real love as you can see
I'm glad it happened to you and me

Love Conquers All

Even though we're miles apart
and may only meet on the beach one time a year

On that special day for years to come
we will fulfill our love to its utmost extent
to last until the next time

For our love will conquer all obstacles in our way
and bring us closer through the miles

And keep us close through the days
until we are together once again

For My Love on Valentine's Day

I'm writing this poem to you
To let you know how I feel
And to tell you once and for all
That my love is real

I could never give you all my love
For you could never hold up its weight
'Cause all the love I have for you
Is more than any man can take

You see, Darling, I love you more each day
Not just now and then
Or when a day is special
And full of joy within

My heart is big and filled with the love
That I have for you
And every day it cries for more
So believe my love is true

My love for you is seasoned
From our Heavenly Father above
And I'm sure he's very proud
That He gave me this lasting love

For you see, Darling, my love for you
Is longer than the end of time
And today I hope to prove to you
Just how much I want you to be mine

Valentine's Day

Valentine's Day is a day for love
For boys and girls alike
A special time to make up
When the family's had a fight

So grab a card and give it
To someone you hold dear
And from the smile that shows
We'll know Valentine's Day is here

Lovers

Chance meetings, secret stares
Letting each other know they care
Fleeting touches as one walks by
If noticed, pretends to be shy
Acting as though they've never met
Remembering things they can't forget
Hunting out the secluded places
Always dark so no one can see their faces
Sneaking kisses in the rain
Always hiding each other's pain
Whispering love words so no one can hear
Talking with eyes that are full of fear
Always stealing every chance
Even if only to get a glance
Knowing soon they'll have to part
Holding each other with their hearts
Afraid of being seen or known
Knowing in their hearts that it's wrong
Concluding they can't go on this way
With each other they cannot stay
Saying good-bye with one last kiss
Swearing to the other "It's you I'll miss"
Maybe soon we'll meet again
If our love is strong, I'm sure we'll win
But for now, they must part
Taking a piece of the other's heart

Broken Dreams

We had our dreams of growing old
With the other always there to hold
But our dreams were shattered; we drifted apart
All of it really broke my heart
I think I'm the one who hurt the most
For you were the one who'd always boast
About how you were such a great man
You know I still don't understand

What about those dreams we made as a kid
The way everyone else always did
For a while I thought we'd see our dreams through
We had a good start; just me and you
But now we have our little boy
The one you said filled your heart with joy
Can you imagine how it's gonna be
For him to grow up with only me
Just because you met another girl
Who flipped you out and made you twirl
Some little tramp from off the street
With great big eyes and smelly feet
It only hurts me because of our son
As he has a battle to be won
With only his mom to lead him on
When it should be you there when he comes home
I really wish it'd been me who'd been untrue
As your son's gonna need you

A Letter of Love

Dearest Darling,

I look at the stars and think of you
Sometimes these thoughts make me feel blue
Because I love you more each day
In my own very special way
For my love I cannot hide
It's bubbling over deep inside
I love you so my little pet
But I can't give it to you, yet
Not in a way that would seem fair
Because you're not always there
So many people keep us apart
And Darling, it's breaking my heart
Some day soon, we'll be together
Never to part; love there forever

High School Love

I remember how you held my hand
Also how you lead the band
How about all those walks downtown
Kissing when no one was around
You always called me teacher's pet
There's so much more I can't forget
How we sat close at football games
You promised our love would stay the same
I remember all the laughs
When we laid out of class
I remember trading high school rings
Promising each other everything
I remember lying in the sand
You told me you wanted to fight for our land
You went off to be a soldier boy
"Come back to me" fill my heart with joy
I love you so, I miss you dear
I really wish that you were here
I'll treasure our memories until you return
In my heart our love will burn
I promise that I'll always be true
For my dear soldier, I love only you

Longing
Out of control
Very happy
Eternity

Love,

Your high school sweetheart

Friendship

Friends

They say friends are forever
Of that I am not sure
Too much left to reason
Too much to endure

One moves away
Another pushes ahead
One gets married
Another one is dead

One is a character
One is a pleasure
One making memories
One is a treasure

One is a wanderer
One stays with you through life
One's happy-go-lucky
One carries you through strife

One's a little lazy
One's full of zest
One greets you smiling
And that's the one I like the best

Especially for Patsy

Hey friend,
Do you realize we've been through hell and back
Excitement's one thing our friendship doesn't lack
I'm so glad we became friends
Yours is the kind that lasts till the end
I'll always remember the day we met
It's a time I'll never forget
We've really had our ups and downs
Remember all those walks up town
How about all the good times we've had
They always seem to overpower the bad
Oh, there were sad moments, too
But we always knew just what to do

There were times it seemed it wouldn't last
But our friendship held steadfast
Through all the trials and the pain
Always staying the same
The way it changed was that it grew
Becoming stronger between us two
We're really more than friends
We're like sisters hand in hand
Helping each other through the roughest spots
Never getting mad over who calls the shots
Happiness is having a friendship that's true
But mostly it's having a friend like you

Friendship

Friendship is something that can be cruel
If you don't follow its golden rules
Never get involved in personal bouts
Like when your family's having outs
If you do, you're sure to lose
So just listen when they sing the blues
Give advice if they need or ask for it
Watch carefully if they're pitching a fit
Never let them lure you in
As you want to be on the side that wins
A friend is someone who only helps so much
When you're away, always keep in touch
Lending an ear; being gentle and kind
Giving the other peace of mind
Friendship can be a wonderful thing
When pleasure is what it brings
It can be dangerous so when in doubt
Don't stick your nose in when it should be out
If it's a real and lasting kind
It will be tied in a forever bind
Ask yourself if you're a true friend
Then make sure you are till the end

A Friend

I have a friend I know real well
But her story's still hard to tell
She's really very bold
And her story goes as told
She had a life she thought was great
As she bore more hurts than any woman should take
Her new life was full and rich
As if sewn tightly with love in every stitch
She had her man whom she loved so well
The rest is really hard to tell
She came home to visit some lifelong friends
While she was there her life seemed to end
It seemed her man had met someone new
And their love was no longer true
Here was one more hurt for her to bear
As her man would no longer be there
But her life must carry on
Because she's not alone
She has a child whom she can love
This was a gift from God above
She'll live for her child and I'm sure one day
Love will again come her way
It will be the everlasting kind
Then she will have peace of mind
She's hurt enough as you can see
This isn't the way life's supposed to be
I know somewhere there's happiness, so she can smile again
And instead of losing, she'll always seem to win

Just Friends

Two people helping each other in a time of need
Only doing what is called a friendly deed
A bond grew between them that can't be replaced
It grew slow at a turtle's pace
It's a bond that can't be broken
And yet it goes unspoken
For you see there are others around

Who wouldn't understand the friendship found
So very many years ago
When life was moving, oh, so slow
No one would ever understand
Why she cares for this man
Everyone would think it wrong
If they knew his feelings were just as strong
About this lady from afar
It seems they met under a star
He was there when she needed someone most
Never once did he brag or boast
She was there to lend a hand
Letting him know he was a great man
When they thought their life was through
Their friendship made their dreams come true
Never once would they regret
Just the fact that they had met

Pabby

For a special friend of mine
Who helped me through a trying time

When my problems seemed so big and great
And I felt I couldn't hold up the weight
You stepped in to lend a helping hand
That's just one of the reasons you're my friend
We both had problems and yet
It was yours; you seemed to forget
You worried more about me and mine
Your only concern was keeping me in line
You've really taught me lots of things
About the pleasures life could bring
If it had not been for you
My world would still be empty and blue
I could never forget you and all the things you did
Guess right now it's better for some things to go unsaid
Just remember your happiness means a lot to me
And I'm hoping happy is what you'll always be
I hope if there's sadness with you it will not stay
As you deserve the finest that life can give away

Odds and Ends

My Own Prayer

Father in Heaven, help me, I can't do it alone
I'm trying so hard to make it home
Lord, I know You're listening and that You'll always care
I also know the promise that You'd always be there
My heart's crying out for You and Your love
My eyes are looking to Heaven above
I need to find the answer so terribly bad
For without Your loving grace, I'll always be sad
There was a time I remember when we walked hand in hand
You were showing me the way through the Promised Land
But somewhere I lost You and I want you again
I can't stand this life that's full of sin
As I've known the extent of Your love
That you sent down from above
Sometimes I look at the stars at night
I rejoice at their sight
Sometimes I feel I can see Your face
And I know that through Your love and grace
I'll soon be back in Your fold
Standing proud, feeling bold
Hear me please; hear my plea
As I don't like the girl that's me

Amen

Autumn and Seasons

Looking out the window and what do I see
Beautiful colors shining back at me
The trees losing leaves one and all
You can tell it's time for Fall
Autumn is a cold time of year
But the colors make it dear
We don't mind the bitter cold
'Cause the trees are pretty standing bold
When the leaves fall it makes me sad
Sometimes the Winters are really bad
But then it's Spring with flowers in bloom
The skies shine with a beautiful moon
Then it's Summer with flowers so bright
Boy, our seasons are really a sight

Winter Time

Winter is a season, I have mixed emotions about
And up until now I hadn't really thought it out
I hate all the clothes that we have to wear
And making sure the blanket's on the old grey mare
I hate the fact it's boring; not much to do
I guess in the Winter I am mostly blue
If you like guessing what the weather is going to be
Then you should like Winter especially
There are a few things to Winter that can be good
Like seeing dad in the big coat with the fur hood
Hot chocolate late at night with a snack or two
A great big fire can take away the blue
But the thing I like best is the flower very dear
That says good-bye to Winter, Spring is finally here

A Good Deed

Trying to be helpful
Is such a hard task
But they tell you
"Hey, I didn't ask"

You knew that your
Intentions were good
And now you're sad
You did all you could

Then your help seems to backfire
Everything stands still
You get a feeling in you
That makes you feel quite ill

You were only doing
What anyone else would do
It seems to turn out wrong
Just because it was you

Maybe it pays to be mean at times
And not lend a hand
Instead of being kind
Maybe you should take a stand

Leave others' problems to themselves
And let them work it out
It'll relieve you of the trouble of wondering
What it's all about

Don't be a friend to everyone
Only those who really care
The ones who, no matter what
For you they'll be there

Get your act together

Is a phrase I always hear
Each and every day
No matter what the year
I haven't figured out yet

If it means put on a play
It's continuously said
Each and every day
I think it means to be

As smart as those
In the working world
You can't worry about runs in your hose
You must keep yourself together

Always keep your cool
In other words
Don't go acting like a fool

Or could it be
That you talk too fast
Oh, wait
I think I've got it at last

It means to cool off
When you're mad
Or does it mean to smile
When you're sad

Some day I'll know
What it means
Maybe it's saying
Keep yourself clean

No sense in trying
To make a guess
As my act's not together
But I'm doing my best

The day I get an answer
I'll let the whole world know
Then we'll get our act together
And be on our toes

Fishing

There we were a-fishing
In Toccoa's Lake
A-trying to catch a fish
I don't think they were awake

It seems we sat there for hours
Without a single bite
One thing is for certain
Those fish stayed out of sight

Oh, I am forgetting
We did catch one small fish
Hopefully the next time
We will get our wish

A seven pound bass
Isn't that what you said
If we don't get it
I'd rather be dead

As to feel the disappointment
Of another trying day
If those fish don't want to be caught
In the lake they shall stay

We'll find another lake
And be glad we went
As we'll come home with a bundle
And know our time was well spent

Pinochle

I learned a new card game
Just the other day
You know cards are good
To pass the time away

The game is called Pinochle
It is lots of fun
Especially when you can brag
You're the team that won

Depressed

I have a suggestion to make
As I've took all I can take
When you're feeling low and depressed
You should lie down and rest

'Cause if you stay
Around your friends
You'll soon be ready
To throw up your hands

And quitting just isn't
Going to work
You should have thought it over
You stupid jerk

I'm sure if you'd thought
Everything would have been all right
Instead, you hung around
And got in a fight

You'd end up making
Enemies of those around
Just because you were hurt
And didn't settle down

You should sit quietly
When you feel like this
And think of the feelings
You might have missed

Go off alone for a while
I think it's best
Especially when
You're really depressed

Think of something
That will make you smile
Then everything
Will be worthwhile

Pregnant Without Marriage

I never really knew
What real love was all about
Until I got pregnant
And had to do without

My parents said I embarrassed
And filled them with shame
They couldn't hold their heads up
And I was to blame

They said I should hide myself
Never go outdoors
As if I were the type
Who could pace the floors

I love this child
More each day
It's not here
It's still on its way

But it's something I'll have
Of my very own
Someone I can love
And provide a home

A life full of pleasure
Is what it'll be for me
And happy is
What I'll always be

Loneliness Is ...

Loneliness is a feeling of deep despair
Being alone with no one who cares
Everywhere you look, the room seems to be closing in
Every time you turn around, you lose instead of win
It's having no one with whom to share
All your thoughts that linger there
You're feeling completely alone
Without love or a home

Loneliness is reaching out for a dream
It's not there; you start to scream
But no one's around to hear
All that's left is to shed a tear
Who would be there to dry your eyes
Just look up to the skies
You're never really all alone
The Lord's always in your home
He can even be in your heart
So why not start
Looking up when you feel bad
You can rest assured you'll never again be sad

Colors

I can't understand people or the way they feel
They're so hostile it can't be real
There's so much hate for each other
Always fighting about the color
Of a person's skin
If it's different, he can't win
There's always a feud between black and white
Even though we know this isn't right
We should realize we're all the same
With feelings, dreams, even our names
No one should be downed for what they are
As that very person may become a star
We should all love each other

As we would a sister or brother
This is true you know
As the Lord told us so
He made us basically alike
So tell me why do we fight
Just because we're not all the same
I think it's an awful shame
Besides, I'd hate to see it, if we all looked alike
But it could be good, we wouldn't know who to fight
We couldn't tell anyone apart
We'd go around hurting our own hearts
So why not show love to everyone
Then we can say we've really won

Silence

Lying here thinking when something comes to mind
It sent a feeling over me that was warm and kind
The thought is that of friendship and something much more
The kind that lasts forever and never becomes a bore
It's such a nice feeling to know someone cares
And as long as you have a friend, there will be someone to share
All your ups and downs as my friend and I have done
We both realize together we have a battle to be won
We were talking earlier about life and all its pain
Of how things are changing and nothing stays the same
We talked of people and how they hurt each other
We feel that all the world should be treated like a brother
It's good that we're not afraid to say how we feel
As we two can be honest and still
We hurt each other by saying what we mean
But at least we're honest and our souls are clean
Well good night my friend; thanks for coming on this day
I'm so glad I asked you to stay

My Vacation

Here I sit by the creek
Camping out in the heat
It's been fun with sights to see
Some a wonder even to me
Canyons and mesas with views galore
Leaving you breathless and wanting more
Camping is a lot of fun
When you find a spot that's not in the sun
Riding around the country makes you feel free
It gives you a good feeling like all life should be
Everyone should take a vacation like my friend and I
Go by car, don't ever fly
You'll miss all the sights and there's plenty to see
You'll also miss the feeling of being free
So the next time you need to leave home
Just get in your car and decide to roam
Go across the hills, deserts, and plains
I promise you'll never feel the same
When you're done you'll be glad you went
You'll know your time was well spent

The Mannequins

Love found them on the street
Only by chance the two should meet
They knew from the knowledge from above
That their feelings were true love
They know it will surely last
You see they're both made of glass

Dedications

Lynn

I remember starting at a new school
I met Deb in class
Little did I know then
How long this friendship would last

She introduced us, I remember
"Karen this is my older sister Lynn"
You said, "If you need help,
I'll be your friend."

Here you were a senior
Freshman were we.
Yet you were conversing with us
how could this be.

You became my best pal
You helped me through some hard times
You always made me feel special
Even when making me toe the line

So thank you my dear friend
For putting up with me twenty years
Through all the laughter
and the many tears

I'll be 4-ever grateful
That we met I have to say
I love you and God Bless You
Forever and a day.

Weaving Trainees

We came to work on Monday
To try and learn a trade
We chose weaving for our skill
Because of the money that can be made

We knew we'd have to face
An instructor for a while
We were nervous, but our minds were put to ease
When she entered with a smile

We were all introduced
And welcomed to the plant
One rule was most important
Never say "I can't"

Our instructor made things seem easy
And explained them simply too
In such a way that we all knew
Exactly what to do

Don't get in a hurry
The looms won't go out the door
If you're having trouble, leave it
Go to the next one on the floor

You can come back to the one left standing
It will be there when you're through
Maybe then you'll take one look
And know exactly what to do

Our instructor builds up our confidence
Saying you can do it if you try
You'll be glad when you learn it
'Cause then the time will fly by

Weaving isn't easy
We knew that from the start
But on bad days don't worry
Or take it to heart

As the next day you may run
A perfect hundred percent
That will make you feel good
And you'll know your time was well spent

An instructor has a rough job
They must have nerves that won't break
Especially if the trainee
Keeps making the same mistake

But they stick by and push you
So that you will learn
They tell you all about
The money you can earn

They say you can make a weaver
If you only apply yourself
They teach you all they know
Until there's nothing left

Then comes the time
You get that job of your own
Remember trainees
You do it for the money you take home

Red

I've met a lot of people
But never have I laughed as hard
As the day you hollered "Hussy"
When I was standing in the yard

There's so much I want to tell you
So many things to say
But my heart is very heavy
And getting in the way

But before I leave my friend
I must unload my heart
To give you something to remember
While we're miles apart

Remember the song "Reach out, touch a hand"
I did, and it gave me a wonderful friend
I know we've had our ups and downs
We've shared a lot of walks up town

Always remember the good times we've had
As they'll always overpower the bad
Think about the tattoos we share
And you'll know that I care

There've been some sad moments, too
But we knew just what to do
We were there for each other
For the happy and the blue

I know I acted different
Even smug and grim at times
But an attitude adjustment
Always put me back in line

We've shared a lot of laughs
And a whole lot of tears
We've got some special memories
To carry us through the years

And now my friend
Before I go away
There's just a few more things
That I have to say

Please remember your happiness
Means a lot to me
And I'm hoping happy is
What you'll always be

If there must be some sadness
I hope it goes away fast
As you've had enough
In the years that've passed

I wish for only the best
Life can give away
Remember I love you forever
And a day

Especially for Mayron

A warm smile on a friendly face
Anger comes out at a turtle's pace
She's hardly ever down
She always waits till no one's around
Her hurt feelings she doesn't show
She walks around all aglow
Brightens up even the darkest day
In her own very special way
Anyone would be lucky to be her friend
As hers is the kind that lasts till the end
Never worry about problems as she's always there
Letting you know that she cares
She fell one day and hurt her foot real bad
But never for a minute was she sad
She trudged on and did all she could
Doing her work as she always would
Even though she should be home in bed
This is exactly what she said
"Must do my work, I can't stop
Just because I have to hop..."

A Nurse

A nurse's duties vary
Sometimes they're good and bad
Sometimes your job's a happy one
Other times it can be sad

Like easing a patient's pain
Taking care of all their hurts
Taking it in stride
When you find one that's a flirt

Like the boy with the winning smile
Or that little girl so dear
Knowing no matter what the outcome
The Lord is always near

He will only do just what
He feels is right
So don't get discouraged
If your patient gives up the fight

Sometimes you'll take your feelings
And lock them on a shelf
You'll give all your time
Until you feel there's none left

But then you'll think about the time
You helped someone to get well
Or about the patient down the hall
With all the great stories to tell

Then it will be worth your efforts
'Cause there's a lot of pleasure in it
And you can wear a smile
Each and every minute

There are some points to ponder
Like not taking a job if you're blue
Let some other nurse have it
Who feels better than you do

As a patient needs all your time
Lots of care and rest
You can't give it to them
If you're not feeling your very best

First impressions are important
Your patient depends on you
They lie in bed resting
And watching what you do

You can change their whole disposition
And nurses that's a fact

So enter the room with a smile
A sweet sound to your voice
You're there because you're needed
And it was your choice

You can be a good nurse
Just look down in your heart
Make sure there's caring feelings
That's where the love of others starts

If you have that you know
That you can win
You're a nurse - one of God's helpers
You'll be rewarded in the end

Vallie

There's a lady at the office
She's very warm and kind
She keeps us all laughing
'Cause she's funny all the time

Her age is fifty-four
But you'd never know it
'Cause she acts so much younger
Besides, her face doesn't show it

She's a special person
Friendly, yes, sirree
She's everyone's kinda friend
We love her defiantly

The day she came to work
We knew our days would be fun
We're glad you're here, Vallie
And that comes from everyone

For Gaylene and Danny

These two would bring a smile to your face
With all their love, devotion, and grace
I'd like to take the time now
To tell you their story and show you how
Devotion can play a very big part
As long as it comes from the heart
They've been through pure torment here
They have the Lord now, Whom they hold dear
But before the Lord entered their hearts
They had so many problems, it seemed they'd fall apart
For a long time she was sick and close to death's door
He worked, hardly slept, sometimes ate lunch at the store
Just to spend all moments with her
Even though there were times she didn't stir
But in her heart his love made her want to pull through
She keeps hearing his words "I'm here so don't be blue"
The day finally came when she was well again
That goes to show you real love always wins
Oh, they had a long wait with lots of bills to pay
But they forgot about them on this day
They only thought of showing their love
'Cause finally they had the piece of a dove
It seemed as though things were looking up
They got an apartment, a car, and even a truck
She laughed so much it filled the room
That once was so unhappy and full of gloom
It was such a great joy to hear this
Something no one would have wanted to miss
It seemed things were better than they ever were
She loved him and he loved her
They spent their time giving the love
The Lord had sent them from above
But then there was a wreck on the highway
That took her loved one far away
Yet neither one is alone
As they have God in their home
He'll see them through as He did before
That's one thing we can be sure

They have the love of family and friends
Soon their hardships will all end
They'll have a life so full and rich
Love sewn in every stitch
The Lord won't let them bear more than they can take
But we have to understand sometimes He makes us wait
So we'll appreciate the happiness He gives
Thanking Him always for coming to live
In our hearts there to stay
Helping us walk the straight way
You see this couple's had it rough
It seemed to them life would always be tough
Then they realized through all the pain and strife
They've had a lot in this life
Oh, they had the problems as you see and yet
The greatness of their love helped them forget
Someday soon they'll be together
They've borne enough, it can't take forever
The Lord promised they'd have happiness in their home
And you know the Lord is never wrong

For Nellie

Nellie is a person whom I've come to know
I'm so glad when she's around and life is all aglow
She's one of God's 'children and yet
She has problems she can't forget
But she strives for others, never herself
She'd give and give until she has nothing left
As she knows she'll be rewarded in the end
'Cause she has Jesus for a friend
I admire her and what she stands for
Never sophisticated, never a bore
Always laughing, never sad
Even when times are really bad
Oh, I've seen her down and out
But then all of a sudden she'd start to shout
About her glory and her praise
As she knows with God there'll be better days
She isn't perfect, God doesn't expect her to be
She has sad moments just like you and me
She has someone to fall back on
Knowing some day He'll carry her home
Away from all the pain and strife
So she'll gladly bear with this life
Even when she isn't well she always says nice things
That's why being her friend always brings
Laughter and a twinkle to the eye
I even believe there's a smile in the sky
The Lord made something in my friend
I hope we're close until the end
I know the Lord's her guidance by day
And never at night would she forget to pray
Thanking Jesus for warmth and love
Sent to us from Heaven above
Knowing the Lord will always be there
So never worry, He'll always care
Always follow the path He chose
Never worry about your clothes
As Jesus only sees what's in your heart
That's the place real love starts

Nellie, I'm glad we met
You're one person I'll never forget

For Teresa and Ricky

I saw them on their wedding day
It was such a sight to behold
Especially when we heard them say
We'll be together even when we're old
They took their vows
Forgetting their pride
Promising to always
Be by each other's side
I watched them through
The tears in my eyes
Everyone there
Began to sigh
At the bride's beauty
And the groom's smiling face
Their love ringing out
All over the place
We watched them walk out
Arm in arm
Promising with their eyes
They'd never see harm
Their love will outshine
All the downs
Even when hard times
Come around
When they left the church
It filled
With smiles and tears
To the gild
At this couple's happiness
The Lord chose to bless
I've seen then a few times
Since that day
And you know
Their love's still the same way

Especially for Billy

A little boy who makes my eyes
Twinkle like the stars in the skies
Since we've met he's brought me joy
Even as I watch him playing with a toy
Sometimes he's in a world all his own
As all children are when they're home
He always has a smiling face
One that shines all over the place
This child filled the loneliness in my heart
Especially since my family and I are so far apart
People mistake us for sister and brother
I guess it's because we favor each other
We're really not related at all
I'm his sitter, just live down the hall
Sometimes I'm mistaken for his mother
So to keep from explaining, I say he's my brother
I really, deep down, wish we were
So in later years our closeness wouldn't become a blur
Billy, I hope you never forget me
I know I want you, just wait and see

For Maggie

I really don't know where to start
Guess I'll let the words come from my heart
You've always been my sunshine on the darkest day
The light at the end of the tunnel showing me the way
You were the most loving, all arms and feet
A smile full of dimples and, oh, so very sweet
Spaghetti O's for lunch, and always before bed
Some kind of story had to be read
Bath time was a pleasure, you giggled very loud
Day dreaming was a must, head always in the clouds
You know when we met you were only five
Your spirit made the house seem to come alive
Over the years you really haven't changed

Except for getting older, you're still the same
It's hard to imagine your being a teen
I hate that I missed the years in between
Thank goodness you still have your great big smile
Guess I'll hang around for a little while
So I can attend graduation, the loudest I will clap
I'm anxious to see how you turn out
You're growing up, Maggie, keep your winning grin
And always remember, I'm glad to be your friend

For Ferrell

Your poetry's endless, you write from the guts
Never has anything gotten to me quite as much
Guess it's because it shows such a serious side
Like an ocean with a furious tide
Keep it up for it expresses you so well
For with it great stories you tell
Your smile is a pleasure to see
A pure treasure it will always be
Your personality is wide and vast
Which puts you at the head of the class
Your writing is serious, it comes from the heart
To write about you isn't an easy part
Guess it's because you have such grace
Never could your friendship be easily replaced
Your youth is so overwhelmingly grand
Beside you is where everyone stands
Frustration is what you sometimes feel
So quiet moments you often steal
Many times I wonder what to do
Wish all days were good for you
You're kind and gentle, always doing good deeds
I'm here for you anytime you need
A shoulder, ear, or a helping hand
Glad you let me be your friend

David

To a guy who brought back my smile
He made everything seem worth while
Before I met him I was down and sad
But he made me see I could be glad
He makes me smile when I'm down the most
And never once would he brag or boast
He laughs a lot and makes jokes
He's right there if you start to choke
To offer any help he can
He really is a great man
He's the type all mothers pray for their girls
Not the kind who'd hurt them, put their world in a twirl
The kind that always seems to be there
Letting you know he'll always care
And to think he chose me to love
It's a miracle from above
I hope I'm worthy of the feelings we share
Do I believe it do I dare
As I've never felt this way before
It's a feeling I'll treasure forever more

Betty

She's like the sunshine, shining so bright
The type of person who fills your heart with delight
I'm so glad that we met
As she's one person I'll never forget
Laughter plays a big part in her home
As a joke she once gave us a bone
She always tries to make the unhappy ones glad
As she doesn't like anyone feeling bad
She'd take a stranger and help them out
She'd take a skinny person and make them stout
She'd give all she had if she thought it would help
She'd show the way step by step
Thinking always of lending a helping hand
This is one lady who's really grand
She always has something nice to say
Make you laugh in her own special way
She's special and I'm glad we're friends
She's the type who'd be there till the end
You never have to wonder if she cares
As she's always around ready to share
In all your problems no matter how great
She'd help you right then, you wouldn't have to wait
She should be nominated Friend of the Year
Because her friendship is so dear
It's the everlasting kind
So you can have peace of mind
As long as we have Betty around
Unhappy moments will never be found
She gives of herself and so much more
I'll tell you what she stands for
Love, friendship, laughter, and cheer
So let's always keep Betty near

Flight W145

We've made it through our six long weeks
We'll be walking proud down the streets
Remembering the time just past
Because we graduated at last
Left! Right! Was loud and clear
Or ladies get your tails in gear
Marching in the boiling sun
Keep in step every one
P.C. in the early morn
Wishing we were in the dorm
Beds made up good and tight
Every one must do it right
Shoes shined to mirror clean
We thought that was awful mean
But they did look good with our blues
It was better than wearing dirty shoes
Everything grounded in other words touch
Would go on but there's too much
Like shoes grounded to the bed
When outside wear a hat on your head
Team work was what pulled us through
It made everything a lot easier to do
Now that it's time to part
Thanks, Tsgt. Carpenter, from our hearts

Dedicated to Flight W145

I know it's hard and not always fun
But remember girls you have a job to be done
Tsgt. Carpenter wants honor flight
You can do it just do everything right
I personally want you to beat the rest
And your guys can, 'cause you're the best
You're already the best flight around
Nowhere else can another be found
Maybe I'll get to see you one day

With all your uniforms on display
Shoes shined to a tee
Just because you're getting a visit from me
Well, I'm still up to my funny stuff
Hope your future days are not too rough
Until I see you guys again
Remember the clue word is to always win
This poem probably doesn't sound too hot
But an experienced poet I am not

"Physey"

Friendship is something that's super
If you have some one to share
All your ups and down with
And know they really care

That my friend is something
That I found in you
When I'm feeling lonely
You're there to pull me through

You've filled my heart with laughter
And you put my mind to rest
I know now there are some good people
And my friend you are the best

I met you on a dreary day
It was raining now and then
But the sun came out suddenly
When you became my friend

Ma

The warmest person that I know
Her face is always aglow
She taught me lots of things
"Grow up and see what the future brings"
That was a line she once said
Or was it something that I read
I accomplished what she wanted me to
I think I've done all she wanted me to do
She tried to be the mother image I needed at the time
Telling me things, but pretending the thoughts were mine
Always telling me to go far
"Who knows, you might even become a star"
She pushed and made me carry on
Letting me know I wasn't alone
She made me want to finish school
"You can't quit like some ole fool"
Getting my diploma was the greatest of all
It was like taking my first step without a fall
Knowing I made my pretend-ma proud
Makes me feel as though I could stand out in any crowd
I'm so glad we two met
The memories something I can't forget
Thanks so much for being there
But mostly for letting me know you care

To the Class of '62

Fifteen years have come to pass
Since we were together last
This isn't a lecture, just words of praise
Remembering the good ole days
Class reunions are so much fun
Finding out what we've all done
I am basically the same
I've gotten married and changed my name
I've had two children a daughter and a son
When they were born I weighed a ton
Me and my slender self
After they were born there wasn't much left
We've all changed and gotten older
Some of us a little bolder
As you can see I'm still being funny
So my days are naturally sunny
I remember as though it were yesterday
Playing a drunk in our senior play
Remembering being voted most popular and wittiest
Through it all I did my best
I look different as I'm sure we all do
Years and age does that to you
It was smart of me to figure that out
I know now what life's all about
It's getting older, wiser, and a reunion with family and friends
And realizing the happy times never had to end
Okay, I'm serious now, it's about time and how
Sorry I couldn't be with you all on this day
But my family and I are going away
We'll be thinking of you all and the years past
Remembering the good times in class
Just don't credit me for this poem I wrote
As it's just another one of my jokes

Telemarketing

I work at a telephone office
We have fun every day
So many different people
To help pass the time away

There's a girl named Debbie
She's good for a laugh
She talks kind of funny
Breaks you in half

There's a guy named Ron
Makes sales all the time
He has a special knack
For keeping people on the line

Rosalee and Henry are closers
Special beyond compare
If there's a sale going on
You're sure to find them there

Sally's the instructor
Who greets you at the door
She tells you enough about the job
To make you want more

Then there's Lisa
She's always on the ball
Handles all your messages
Accepts all your calls

Beverly arrives
When the shift is almost done
She always comes in
Smiling at everyone

George arrives yelling
"Come on gang rock and roll"
Helga pushes sales
With her very soul

Rhana is a princess
Larry is a clown

And of course we're glad
Geneals back in town

Brenda is our dresser
JoAnn smiles a lot
Latka's the one
Who stays in his spot

J.T. and Steve
They like to compete
And I'm the one they wish
Would stay in her seat

But you know talking on the telephone
Is such a hard task
Especially selling something
You have to talk real fast

As they can't see
Who's on the other end
That's why selling
Is awful hard my friend

So get your pitch
Across real quick
Before your party
Starts getting sick

When they realize
They just made a buy
All because
They let you say "Hi"

You'll leave with
A smile on your face
To know your day
Wasn't a waste

'Cause you made some sales
Commissions galore
So smile when you
Go out the door

Make sure you're there everyday
So you can grab all that PAY! PAY! PAY!

Shari

A new girl at the office
We must, mention here
Her story's special
Filled with laughter and a tear

She sat quietly for a week
Defiantly having a losing streak
Seven days had come to pass
Then the sales were coming fast

Staying power's the reason
This story's being told
No telling how many
Deals she has sold

All because she didn't give in
She can leave with a happy grin

Henry

There's a guy at the office named Henry
He's like a father to every one
He treats the girls with kindness
The guys as though his sons

He's a delightful supervisor
He brightens the darkest day
If you're just starting he handles you
In a very special way

He makes the job much easier
He lifts your spirit as he walks the floor
But the greatest thing about him
Is his smile when you walk through the door

He very much deserved the promotion
A closer we all hold dear
So cheers to you, Henry
We're sure glad you're here

McDonald's®

Fast foods are here to stay
And here you can have it your way
Bring your family, come one, come all
We at McDonald's® are on the ball
We always greet you with a smile
If you wait, it's only for a little while
We'll bring it to you so have a seat
We'll apologize for the wait and smile real sweet
Our production caller watches for a crowd
When one comes he starts calling loud
Regulars on the turn
Something all grill hands must learn
The killers are Quarters and McD's
They're done perfect, we aim to please
Suddenly a shout "Here comes a bus"
If the customer could see they'd laugh at us
We're running around like little chicks
Everything has to be done real quick
We serve breakfast in the early morn
This is the place the egg mac was born
Come for supper or early lunch
Grab an apple pie to munch
Salads are good for a midday snack
Don't forget our great Big Mac
How about nuggets, they won't hurt
Or shakes and sundaes for dessert
We have everything for a meal
Even have coupons for a good deal
Our work is hard so it seems
That's 'cause we're a winning team
As long as you want it, your job will last
'Cause everyone loves food that's fast
So find a McDonald's®, there's always one near
And thanks for coming, "Ya'll come back now, ya hear!"

Especially for Iva

You're very special
In a unique sort of way
There's so many things
That I'd like to say

Working with you is a pleasure
Words just can't express
You fill the day with laughter
Makes us try to do our best

A good friend is something
That I have in you
When I'm feeling down
You're there to pull me through

When the job is going badly
And very hard to bear
It always seems much easier
Whenever you are there

Thanks for the encouragement
The laughter and the smiles
Especially the hugs and compliments
You make the day worth while

Iva, I'm always hoping
You're never ever blue
As you deserve all the happiness
Life can give to you

Always remember
When the day is at an end
That I will always be
Your "little" friend

Keela

I remember meeting
You at the show
You're one person
I'm glad I know

And now you're moving
In just another day
There's so much more
That I'd like to say

Words are hard to come by
When you're feeling sad
But if it'll make you happy
I'll try to be glad

You've brought so much laughter
To this house of gloom
Hopefully you'll come visiting
Last week wouldn't be too soon

You'll be missed by everyone
A sadness hangs overhead
There's still a lot more
That needs to be said

You're someone special
A friend so very dear
Boy I'm gonna miss
Not having you here

Take care of yourself
Find what it is you need
You're of the highest quality
Yes, my friend, indeed

Don't get discouraged
Be all that you can be
Always remember
You have a friend in me

Especially for Tina

Fifteen years have come to pass
Since we saw each other last

Our meeting was for sadness
The reason wasn't good
I tried to make it happy
As best I could

I've thought about you often
And missed you very much
From now on please promise
We'll always keep in touch

Friendship is a special family
All its very own
Ours started in our childhood
And continued as we've grown

We're really like sisters
Much more than friends
So ours will last a lifetime
Like a ring that has no end

I hope you know
Just how much I care for you
And if you ever need anything
You can count on me, too

Urgent!!

A Message to Families

Watching home movies, memories from the past
God, why couldn't those times have last

Looking at the closeness we shared
A time when everyone really cared

Lots of smiles, happy faces galore
Even a few sad ones to explore

It seems we were more than kin
I think we were all really good friends

So what happened as we grew
We drifted apart as people often do

So our children together will never play
As we did on those sunny days

They should be close as we were then
That's the way it should have been

So much to say, but where to start
As I sit here with a heavy heart

I'll just say: See if any of this applies to you
And think about what you should do

"Always say how you feel, don't ever wait
As one day it may be too late"....

From someone who will care from now 'til the end
Just someone with a message to send

A Testimonial for Jerry

They say we're not to question
The reason or the why
Yet this is one time
I have to say with a sigh

Lord, why did you have to let
Jerry be taken away
Guess the answer is
We'll understand some day

He was taken by the hand of another
And that's the very part
That we need answered
'Cause, Lord, it breaks our hearts

I tell myself it was because
You were ready to call him home
And yet someone else took his life
And that's why he's gone

All these unanswered questions
Lord, it isn't right
I apologize for my wonder
As I look into the night

Jerry, we will miss you
With each passing day
Thanks, Lord, for listening
And letting me have my say

Kathy's Story

People often say three strikes you're out
For me that wasn't true
Third time was a charm
That's when I got you

Our love had burned inside me
For fifteen long, hard years
I dreamed of what we lost
And have shed many tears

I was devastated
My heart was filled with pain
I prayed every day
For this not to be done in vain

If our parents had left us alone
Let our love for each other grow
Together there's no telling
Just how far we would go

Relationships didn't come easy
Thoughts of you burned within
I saw something of you
In all the other men

You know you're my best friend
My love grows more with each day
Love that was put on hold
Grew in its own special way

People say we're a special couple
You know they are right
I wish we could turn the clock back
I'd sure put up a fight

No one will ever know how I suffered
Thoughts of you set me on fire
It burned and smouldered deep within
As I dreamed of my heart's desire

They say youthful love is only make believe
A fairytale or dream
Well ours was all of these to me
And came true so it seems

Sandy

You know from the time we met
I knew you were a friend
I knew it would be a friendship
Like a ring that has no end

You make me feel important
Like there's a purpose after all
No reason to be afraid
I think you'd catch me if I fall

I hope you'll share in my glory
My disappointments too
'Cause the biggest major step
Was made partly because of you

You see you've been an inspiration
A friend beyond compare
It's almost like having a sister
Thanks for being there

Now thank yourself for pushing me
In the direction that I chose
Where I'll go from here
Heaven only knows

But no matter where I go
Or what my future sees
I want you to be there
To share it all with me

He Came to Me

(He Holds the Key)

Standing on the corner
Who did I see
Jesus was there
Looking back at me

He said, "My child
I can see what's been done
You've been caught up in the world of sin
And think you're having fun"

Chorus

Jesus is the Master
He holds the key
To a great salvation
He's offered it to me

And through His great love
We can all be set free
Just call on Jesus
For He holds the key

While walking down this darkened road
Feeling sad and all alone
Jesus was there once again
Saying,"Child, I'll carry you home"

He said, "Take my hand
We'll walk real slow
Put all your trust in Me
We don't have far to go"

Chorus

Jesus is the Master
He holds the key
To a great salvation
He's offered it to me

And through His great love
We can all be set free
Just call on Jesus
For He holds the key

I took that walk with Jesus
What did I have to lose
He showed me the plan of salvation
It was now my turn to choose

I'm thankful He was on that corner
I accepted Him that day
Yes, I know He's real
He is the only Way

Chorus

Jesus is the Master
He holds the key
To a great salvation
He's offered it to me

And through His great love
We can all be set free
Just call on Jesus
For He holds the key